1. Introduction

Large banks use internal estimates of credit risk to calculate the capital that they must hold. Under the Basel II and Basel III regulatory rules, the capital that banks are required to hold is designed to align closely with the credit risk of specific assets on banks' books by relying upon banks' ability to assess this risk. In particular, risk-based capital requirements for internationally active large banks depend on their internal estimates of key risk parameters, including the probability of default (PD) — the likelihood that a borrower will not be able to repay in full over one year — and the loss given default (LGD) — the portion of funds that the bank expects to lose when a borrower defaults within a one-year horizon during an economic downturn.

A prominent concern about this approach is that if the risk parameters that banks use do not measure risk accurately, banks will hold an insufficient or an excessive amount of capital. Unfortunately, because the available data are limited, we cannot ascertain whether internally generated PDs and LGDs are close to the true PDs and LGDs of most assets. Still, we can identify which banks, if any, most likely underestimate or overestimate these parameters by investigating whether internal estimates of risk parameters differ systematically across banks. That is, do some banks report risk parameters that, on average, are lower or higher than those reported by other banks for similar exposures?

In this paper, we analyze whether the PDs and the LGDs that nine of the largest internationally active U.S. bank holding companies assign to one key asset class — syndicated commercial and industrial (C&I) loans — differ systematically across these banks, that is, if they are consistent across banks.[1] In May 2011, the Federal Reserve Board (Fed) surveyed these banks and they reported their internal estimates of PDs and LGDs for syndicated C&I loans that they held in their portfolios as of the survey date.[2] Most loans in the survey were fully funded term loans with standard repayment schedules extended to large U.S. public companies.

---

[1] In order to protect the confidential nature of supervisory information, we do not identify the banks in our sample. Also, for simplicity, we refer to bank holding companies as banks.
[2] Exposure at Default (EAD), which reflects banks' forecasts of likely usage of credit lines at the time of default, and Maturity (M), which reflects banks' forecasts of how long until a loan terminates, are two other parameters that affect risk-based capital requirements. If estimates of EAD or M are correlated with estimates of PD and LGD

We exploit two key features of syndicated loans that help us understand the extent to which internal estimates of risk parameters differ systematically across banks. First, we use data on loans that were held by at least two banks. This allows us to isolate the systematic differences across banks in the risk parameters that they assign to the loans, the metrics we are interested in estimating, from the effects of unobservable characteristics of loans on these parameters, features that may confound our estimates. Second, each bank's income or loss from a syndicated loan is proportional to its share of the loan, independently of its role in the syndicate. Thus, any systematic differences in banks' PDs and LGDs for an identical portfolio of syndicated loans across banks cannot be caused by loan characteristics.

We find that the nine banks in our sample differ substantially in PDs, but only a few differ from the median bank systematically in the same direction, which conforms with previous results from the literature (for example, Carey, 2002). However, most banks differ systematically in LGDs and two of them deviate substantially from their counterparts: one bank assigns LGDs on average 12.79 percentage points lower than the median bank and another bank assigns LGDs 17.44 percentage points higher than the median bank. As Basel II regulatory capital requirements depend on LGDs, these differences imply that the minimum regulatory capital of these banks differ by large magnitudes. We estimate that, under mild assumptions, the bank that systematically sets the highest LGDs would have a minimum regulatory capital twice as large as the capital of the bank that sets the lowest LGDs for the same portfolio of loans.

However, we note that a feature of the Basel rules is that banks can have legitimate differences in opinions and approaches to managing and measuring credit risk, which can cause differences in risk parameters across banks. Thus, the true PD or LGD of a loan could in fact vary across banks, and banks would then diverge on the risk parameters that they assign to the same loan for legitimate reasons, which are unrelated to a systematic bias by some banks. Indeed, we find a negative relation between banks' estimates of LGD and their shares in loan syndicates, which suggests that the systematic differences that we find in LGDs actually represent differences in losses that banks expect to incur if their borrowers default on their loans. This finding also

---

across banks, then differences in estimates of EAD and M can offset or reinforce differences in PD and LGD. However, data on EAD or M were not available, so they are excluded from this analysis.

indicates that our results on systematic differences in risk parameters across banks potentially have implications for other topics besides bank capital, such as the relation between loan supply and dispersion of beliefs about risk.

This paper contributes to the literature on banks' internal credit ratings. This literature mostly analyzes how banks rate borrowers and loans and how banks use their internal ratings (Brady, English, and Nelson, 1998; Elsas and Krahnen, 1998; English and Nelson, 1998; Machauer and Weber, 1998; Treacy and Carey, 2000; Grunert, Norden, and Weber, 2005). Our paper is closely related to RMA Capital Working Group (2000), Carey (2002), Jacobson, Lindé, and Roszbach (2006), and Financial Services Authority (2012), which investigate whether banks' internal credit ratings are consistent across banks. Among these four papers, the closest to ours are RMA Capital Working Group (2000) and Financial Services Authority (2012). As in our paper, RMA Capital Working Group (2000) uses a sample of syndicated loans to examine if the PDs that banks assign to loans are consistent across banks. Alternatively, Carey (2002) and Jacobson, Lindé, and Roszbach (2006) use samples of borrowers – instead of samples of syndicated loans - to examine if the internal ratings that banks assign to loans – instead of PDs - are consistent across banks. Financial Services Authority (2012) is, as far as we know, the only study besides ours to examine whether LGDs are consistent across banks. However, RMA Capital Working Group (2000) and Financial Services Authority (2012) only use descriptive statistics to study this question, while we also use econometric evidence.

We also contribute to the literature on syndicated loans and information asymmetry. This literature has studied how information asymmetry determines syndicate structure (Dennis and Mullineaux, 2000; Lee and Mullineaux, 2004; Sufi, 2007), loan prices in secondary markets (Allen and Gottesman, 2006), loan spreads (Ivashina, 2009), and loan contract features (Drucker and Puri, 2009). Our paper is closely related to Dennis and Mullineaux (2000), Lee and Mullineaux (2004), and Sufi (2007), which show that the share of loans that banks hold varies with information asymmetry. We contribute to this literature by showing how loan shares vary across banks depending on their risk parameters, which banks estimate using their limited information about borrowers.

This paper is organized as follows. Section 2 describes the data. Section 3 presents our empirical strategy and our results on risk parameter dispersion. Section 4 discusses the implications of the results for the Basel II minimum regulatory capital required from banks. Section 5 presents additional results on the relation between risk parameters and loan shares. Section 6 concludes.

2. Data

Our dataset combines information from the Thomson Reuters LPC's DealScan database with internal corporate credit risk data from banks. These internal data were collected by the Fed from nine large U.S. bank holding companies in May 2011. The Fed collected these data to better understand these banks' estimates of Basel II minimum regulatory capital for corporate credit risk and to guide additional supervisory work. At the time of data collection they were all in or approaching 'parallel run,' a period during which banks adopt the Advanced Internal Ratings-Based (AIRB) approach to calculate Basel II minimum regulatory capital, but their minimum regulatory capital is still determined by Basel I rules.[3] Banks cannot exit parallel run and start using their internal estimates of risk parameters to calculate capital requirements until regulators approve them, and none of these banks have yet been approved.

DealScan contains information on loans to large firms, including characteristics of each loan contract, its lenders, and its borrower. Contract characteristics include the loan type, loan amount, and the total amount of the deal.[4] Lenders' characteristics include their identity and participation in specific credit facilities. Borrowers' characteristics include their annual sales and

---

[3] U.S. banks above an asset size threshold are required to participate in the AIRB process, while other U.S. banks can choose whether or not to participate. The asset threshold is consolidated total assets of $250 billion or more, as reported on the most recent year-end regulatory reports; or consolidated total on-balance sheet foreign exposure of $10 billion or more at the most recent year end.

[4] The loan amount and the total amount of the deal are equal if the contract contains only one facility. Otherwise, the loan amount is lower than the total amount of the deal. Many deals contain, for example, a term loan and multiple lines of credit with different maturities.

an indicator of whether they are a public firm rated by Moody's or S&P, a public nonrated firm, or a private firm.[5]

For each of the nine banks, the Fed created a subsample of loans restricting the DealScan data to loans that the banks had actually extended either by themselves or as part of a syndicate. Loans were eliminated from these subsamples if DealScan reported that they had matured. The final lists of loans submitted to banks were restricted to 500 loans each to limit the burden that this request would impose on banks. Most banks had fewer than 500 loans in the DealScan data, and therefore this limit was not reached by them. For banks with more than 500 facilities remaining in the list, 500 of them were randomly selected for the final lists. When banks extended multiple facilities to a borrower, one of these loans was randomly selected to be included, while others were eliminated from the sample.

The Fed sent to each bank its respective list of loans, with information about each loan, including borrower name, ticker (when available), loan currency, loan type, and contract start and end dates to aid banks in identifying the respective loans. Each bank reported the status of each loan in its list; namely, if it was currently in the bank's portfolio, was sold, had matured, was paid off, was in default, was terminated by any other reason, or simply if it had never been part of the portfolio. For every loan that was currently held in the bank's portfolio, the bank reported the PD and the LGD that it used to calculate Basel II minimum regulatory capital as well as whether or not the loan was secured by some sort of collateral.[6] Banks were asked to report only the most recent PD and LGD for each loan. We eliminated loans with missing PD or LGD from the data reported by banks. Also, from the remaining 1,353 loans, we eliminated those with valid PD and LGD estimates from only one bank, because, based on our empirical strategy, these loans would not help to determine whether banks' risk parameters are consistent. Table 1 shows the distribution of number of banks that provided data about the same loan. The data contain 659 loans. For most of these loans, the data include risk

---

[5] DealScan has been used extensively in past academic research. See, for example, Güner (2006), Sufi (2007) and Ivashina (2009).

[6] DealScan contains information about whether loans are secured or not, but the field is not completely populated. In addition, unsecured loans sometimes become secured after origination due to renegotiation or covenant violations.

parameters from two banks. The maximum number of banks that reported valid parameters for the same loan is equal to seven.

The unit of observation in our analysis is a loan-bank pair and the final sample that we use contains 1,795 observations. The nine banks and the 659 loans are combined in these pairs. The number of loans per bank ranges from 25 to 331 loans, with a median of 210 loans.[7] Table 2 shows descriptive statistics for these loans. Loan amounts are mostly large, with a median of $500 million, and borrowers are large companies too, with median annual sales of $2.74 billion. 62.37 percent are public companies rated by Moody's or S&P, 33.84 percent are public nonrated firms, 1.67 percent are private firms, and for the remaining 2.12 the DealScan data do not contain this information. For some loans, banks contradicted each other on whether these loans were secured by some sort of collateral or not, which requires that we interpret this information carefully. For 93 out of the 659 loans in our sample, at least one bank reported that the loan was secured and at least one bank reported that it was not secured. Among the 566 loans with no conflicting information, 27.39 percent were reported as being secured. However, even among loans with no conflicting information, we do not know how reliable this information is.

Table 3 presents the data specific to each loan-bank pair. Banks lead the loan syndicate in approximately one quarter of these pairs. Banks had previously extended credit to the borrower for 78.38 percent of lender-borrower pairs in the sample. In 27.58 percent of the pairs, the lender had acted as lead arranger for the borrower in a syndicated deal. The median PD is 0.36 percent and the median LGD is 40.70 percent of the exposure amount.

As a first step in the analysis, Figures 1 and 2 show the differences between the PDs and the LGDs assigned by all the 1,868 pairs of banks that participate in the same loan. The bars in Figure 1 show the distribution of the absolute difference between PDs; they range from zero to hundreds of basis points, but most are closer to zero. As shown by the dashed vertical line, about half of the pairs of PDs assigned to the same loan by different banks lie within 17 basis

---

[7] While banks were asked for data on up to 500 loans, some credits had been sold or terminated after origination and prior to the data collection date.

points of each other. Still, the median difference across pairs of banks is relatively large compared with the median PD of 36 basis points, shown in the inset box. Moreover, as shown by the right-most bar, in more than 10 percent of these pairs, PDs differ by more than 100 basis points.

The bars in Figure 2 show the distribution of the differences between LGDs for the same loans across the same pairs of banks. The LGD differences range from zero to almost 60 percentage points, and, similar to differences in PDs, most differences in LGDs are closer to zero: as shown by the dashed vertical line, in roughly half of the pairs, LGDs assigned to the same loan by different banks lie within 13 percentage points of each other. Still, that difference is about one-third of the median LGD of 41 percentage points. Overall, this first cut of the data suggests that the banks' internal assessments of these parameters differ materially and warrant further investigation.

3. Risk Parameter Dispersion

In this section, we investigate what determines the risk parameters that banks assign to loans and, in particular, whether some banks systematically set higher or lower PDs and LGDs than others. We first present our empirical strategy, and then we present and discuss our results.

3.1 Empirical Strategy

We use the following regression to investigate what determines banks' risk parameters:

$$Y_{ij} = X_{ij}\beta + \gamma_i + \delta_j + \varepsilon_{ij}, \qquad (1)$$

where Y_{ij} is the PD or the LGD assigned to loan i by bank j, X_{ij} is a vector of characteristics specific to each loan-bank pair ij and β is a vector of coefficients. γ_i and δ_j are vectors of loan and bank dummy variables, respectively, and ε_{ij} represents an unobservable error specific to each loan-bank pair. We estimate robust standard errors and we cluster observations at the loan level.

We focus on the bank dummies, represented by the vector δ_j. They represent the systematic effect of bank j's approach to estimating PD or LGD. The data contain observations from loans from nine banks, and thus the vector δ_j is composed of eight dummy variables. We leave the bank with the median dummy coefficient estimate as the reference group. Thus, by construction, four of these coefficient estimates are negative and four are positive. The median bank risk parameter is a natural choice for a benchmark given that we investigate if some banks' PDs and LGDs deviate from others' in one direction systematically.[8] The order of banks' dummy coefficient estimates often differs between specifications even for the same dependent variable, and thus each bank does not necessarily rank the same across different specifications. In terms of presentation, this means that each bank dummy number (or row) does not necessarily refer to the same bank across different columns of the tables of results in the paper. We intentionally do not assign a fixed number to each bank across the paper to use the median bank's estimates as the reference case in every specification.[9]

The vector X_{ij} contains three dummy variables: the first indicates whether bank j is a leader in loan i's syndicate, the second indicates whether bank j had participated in a loan syndicate for borrower $k(i)$ in the past, and the third indicates whether bank j led a syndicate for borrower $k(i)$ in the past, where $k(i)$ denotes the borrower who took loan i.[10] This vector, however, does not control for other types of relationship between the bank and the borrower. For instance, the bank may learn more about a firm's ability to repay a loan if the bank also manages cash for the firm. Also, the vector X_{ij} does not control for the relation between loan i and the rest of bank j's portfolio. In theory, a bank could consider how a particular loan

---

[8] Such an approach is similar to Carey's (2002), who reports average differences of each lender's PDs relative to the rest of the sample on Table 6 of his paper. The median is useful because risk parameters are typically asymmetrically distributed, and especially, because PDs and LGDs are large for certain loans. If we knew the true PD and LGD from the loss distribution, using the true parameters would be a better alternative. However, given that we do not know the true parameters, we believe that the median bank risk parameter is the best available benchmark.
[9] This approach also helps to protect the participating banks' identities.
[10] We base this on DealScan. Thus, any relationship not reflected in loans covered by DealScan represents measurement error.

correlates with the rest of its portfolio when measuring credit risk, and this could determine the risk parameters that the bank assigns to that loan.[11] However, the AIRB approach mandates measuring PD and LGD for each loan as an isolated asset, and we assume that banks abide by this requirement.

γ_i is a vector of 658 loan facility dummies, because we limited our sample to the 659 syndicated loans for which we have risk parameters from at least two banks. By including dummies for each loan, we are able to control for unobservable loan characteristics, and thus to identify the impact of differences in banks' risk parameter estimation on these parameters.

3.2 Results

Table 4 shows the regression results using PD as the dependent variable. Column 1 shows the results using the whole sample. Only three out of the eight bank dummies are statistically significant at the 5 percent level. The sample median of PD is equal to 0.36 percent, while the three statistically significant dummy coefficients – the largest number of significant dummies across the different subsamples used in this table – are equal to -0.62, -0.33 and 0.45. This implies a very large effect on these banks' PD estimates. However, these coefficients are only a bit more than one tenth of one standard deviation of PDs in the sample, which is 4.19 percent. We also note that the R-squareds for these regressions are small. Thus, bank dummies together with other controls can only explain a small fraction of the variation of PD estimates.

In the other columns of this table, we investigate if the results change across different subsamples. We first analyze if the results vary with borrower size, here measured by firm sales. Columns 2 and 3 show the results for loans to borrowers with annual sales below and above the median, equal to $ 2.74 billion. None of the bank dummies are significant at the 5

---

[11] See Ivashina (2009) for a discussion of measuring an asset's credit risk covariance with a bank's overall portfolio using DealScan data.

percent level in Column 2, and only one is significant in Column 3, with a coefficient estimate of 0.53. The results, therefore, do not differ substantially between smaller and larger borrowers.[12]

We next investigate if the results vary with borrowers' transparency. We separate the sample depending on whether the borrower is a public firm rated by Moody's or S&P (Column 4) or it is a nonrated public firm or a private one (Column 5). We separate observations in these two groups for two reasons. First, public rated firms are typically viewed as more transparent than nonrated public firms and private firms in syndicate lending (Dennis and Mullineaux, 2000; Lee and Mullineaux, 2004; Sufi, 2007).[13] Second, loans to private firms correspond to only 1.67 percent of the loans in our data, and therefore could not be used as a standalone category in this study. In the sample of PDs of loans to public rated borrowers, three out of the eight bank dummy coefficients are significant and these coefficients also imply large systematic differences in PDs across banks. For example, the lowest and the highest coefficient, equal to -0.79 and 0.73 imply that the PDs assigned by the respective banks to the same loans differ systematically by 1.52 percent, which is large compared to the sample median of PDs of 0.36 percent and even to the sample mean of 1.43 percent. On the other hand, in the sample of PDs of loans to public nonrated and private borrowers, none of the dummies are significant. These results suggest that banks diverge more on PDs of loans to public rated firms, which would be unexpected because these firms should be more transparent, but the smaller number of observations of loans to public nonrated and private firms (600 observations of 234 loans) compared to the number for public firms (1,195 observations of 425 loans) can partially explain the result. In any case, bank dummies and the other independent variables still cannot explain much of the variation of PD estimates across banks and loans.

In Columns 6 and 7, we estimate Equation (1) with the subsamples of secured and unsecured loans, respectively. As we discuss in Section 2, information from banks on whether the

---

[12] These results contrast with those from Carey (2002), who finds that lenders are more likely to disagree in the ratings of smaller borrowers. This difference in results can be explained by a variety of reasons, but the most likely are the differences in the samples used in the two papers and the fact that he studies disagreements in ratings while we study differences in PD estimates.

[13] This criterion, based on Dennis and Mullineaux (2000), Lee and Mullineaux (2004), and Sufi (2007), relies on the assumption that third-party credit ratings and Securities and Exchange Commission filings reduce information asymmetries.

respective loan is secured or unsecured may be incorrect for some loans even after we eliminate loans with conflicting information. Still, all observations that we use in columns 6 and 7 are from loans with no conflicting information, and we rely on these observations to investigate if there are any differences in the consistency of PDs between these two subsamples. For secured loans, we find that some bank dummy coefficients are large, but only one of them – equal to 2.10 – is significant, possibly because of the small sample size. For unsecured loans, we do not find any evidence that other banks diverge systematically from the median bank.

We next investigate if our results depend on loan risk. In columns 8 and 9, we estimate Equation (1) with the subsamples of loans with Moody's senior debt ratings of Baa2 or worse and of Baa1 or better, respectively. We choose these ratings as the threshold to separate the data into two subsamples with the same number of loans, 198. In the sample of loans with low ratings, one bank dummy is significant, while in the sample of loans with high ratings, none of the dummies are significant. Once again, the majority of banks in the two subsamples do not seem to deviate systematically from the median bank.

As a whole, the results in this table imply that the large majority of banks do not diverge systematically in the same direction relative to others in their estimates of PDs. These findings are similar to results from Carey (2002), based on a different sample of lenders and borrowers.

Table 5 shows the results with LGD as the dependent variable. In Column 1, we use the whole sample. The results show that banks differ systematically in their LGD estimates. Seven out of the eight bank dummy coefficients are significant at the 5 percent level. Two of these coefficients, equal to -12.79 and 17.44, imply that the respective banks deviate substantially from the median bank. Most dummies' absolute values vary from three to six percent, which also imply small deviations from the median given the standard deviation of 12.85 percent. The R-squareds for these regressions are higher than in Table 4, suggesting that bank dummies and other independent variables explain more of the variation of LGDs than of PDs.

The results also indicate that banks set lower LGDs to loans extended to borrowers that they led a syndicate for in the past, which may possibly be due to a causal effect. The -1.68

coefficient of the dummy for past leader is small, but statistically significant. It is consistent with Fama's argument that banks obtain private information about firms by lending to them (Fama, 1985). Banks possibly learn about the credit quality of the borrowers that they lead a syndicate for and use this information to screen these borrowers out when they apply for new loans. Therefore, if banks are more likely to extend loans to the safest repeated borrowers, then repeated borrowers should have a lower LGD on average than new borrowers. Such a causal effect might contribute to the empirical regularity that borrowers tend to choose banks that led loan syndicates for them in the past, which was documented by Dennis and Mullineaux (2000), Allen and Gottesman (2006) and Ivashina (2009). However, even though this estimate is consistent with such causal relationship, it does not prove this causal effect. Indeed, the estimate may also result from unobservable characteristics of loan-bank pairs that determine both the LGDs that banks assigned to these loans and whether banks lead syndicates for the respective borrowers in the past. For instance, banks' ability to recover losses from certain types of loans may determine both the LGDs that they assign to those types of loans and their willingness to extend them. Also, a bank that led a syndicate for a firm in the past may be more likely to provide other services (such as cash management or securities underwriting) to it than other banks, which would also help the bank obtain private information about the firm and then affect the LGD that the bank assigns to a loan to this firm. Therefore, we remain skeptical that a causal relation is driving this result.

We again study if the findings above depend on borrower size. As in the previous table, Columns 2 and 3 present the results for borrowers with annual sales below and above the median, respectively. These results are similar to those when we use the whole sample. Most bank dummies are significant in both columns and their sizes are similar too, implying that, independently of borrower size, banks differ substantially in the LGDs that they assign to loans. The results of the two subsamples differ mainly in that the model explains much more of the variation in LGDs of large borrowers compared to smaller ones. Such evidence is consistent with the hypothesis that banks have more information about large borrowers, and so the idiosyncratic variation in LGDs should be smaller.

The results are also similar to those in the first column for both loans to public rated firms and loans to public nonrated or private firms, as shown in Columns 4 and 5, respectively. The coefficients on banks dummies have similar sizes and again imply substantial differences in LGDs across banks. The regression fit is higher for public rated borrowers, which is expected given that these firms are more transparent than the rest, and therefore banks should disagree less on their LGDs.

The findings are also robust when we divide loans between secured and unsecured loans in Columns 6 and 7, respectively. Once again, bank dummies indicate large systematic differences in LGDs across banks. The regression fit is much higher for unsecured than for secured loans, possibly because of uncertainty about the value of the collateral pledged in secured loans, or because there is inherently more disagreement about the risk of secured loan borrowers, which might be a reason why these loans had to be secured.

Columns 8 and 9 show that results are similar to those in Column 1 when we separate the sample by loan ratings too. The results do not differ significantly between columns 8 and 9 and they also imply that systematic differences in LGDs are large across banks.

In summary, the results of this subsection indicate that only a few banks differ systematically from the median bank in the PDs that they assign to loans, but most banks differ systematically in LGDs, independently of loans' characteristics. Thus, it would be natural to ask why the evidence indicates that banks' PDs are similar on average, but their LGDs are not. We discuss potential answers to this question next.

3.3 Differences between Dispersion of PDs and LGDs

We believe that the following are the four main possible reasons for the weaker evidence that PDs differ systematically across banks, compared to the evidence for LGDs:

First, the distributions of PDs and LGD differ substantially. Table 3 shows that the mean of PDs is almost four times as large as the median, while the mean and the median of LGDs are very similar. Accordingly, the standard deviation of PDs is roughly three times as large as the mean, while the standard deviation of LGDs is approximately one third of the mean. Thus, it is possible that many banks' PD estimates actually differ systematically from the median bank's, but their respective dummies are not significant because of the huge dispersion in the distribution of PDs. To investigate whether observations with large PDs, which drive this dispersion, also cause the low significance of bank dummies, in the Appendix we estimate the regression from Table 4 using only observations with PDs below certain values. We also estimate that regression using the natural logarithm of PD as the dependent variable, which may better account for extreme values of PDs, as opposed to the PD in percentage points. However, we still find that only a few banks' PD estimates differ systematically from the median bank's. Thus, even though the large dispersion in PDs may potentially explain the different results for PDs and LGDs, the evidence that we have does not allow us to conclude that this is the main cause for the difference.

Second, banks have more information on PDs than on LGDs. To estimate PDs, large banks typically use their own data on current, delinquent, and defaulted loans, but to estimate LGDs, banks can only use data on losses from defaulted loans. Also, some banks have limited experience with losses, either because they tend to sell off loans prior to default or simply have conservative portfolios in which borrowers rarely default. Banks often compare LGDs that they estimate with their own data against LGDs based on proprietary data sets, such as S&P's LossStats and Moodys' Ultimate Recovery Data, but even these data sets contain a relatively small number of defaulted loans, as opposed to bond defaults. Thus, the systematic dispersion in LGDs may result from lack of data.

Third, besides using internal and external data to estimate risk parameters, banks also compare their parameter estimates with those from rating agencies. However, these agency benchmarks also provide information mostly on PDs, not LGDs. At least for publicly rated firms, there is an easily available third party benchmark for PDs, but until recently there was no such resource available for LGDs. For PDs, Moody's estimates expected default frequencies for many public firms, which is roughly equivalent to a 'point-in-time' default probability, and it is common industry practice to use historic default rates from a rating-agency as a benchmark 'through the cycle' PD measure for rated firms. For LGDs, Standard and Poor's has recently created a 'Recovery Rating,' which could provide a benchmark for corporate LGDs. If banks have used more PD benchmarks than LGD benchmarks, then these rating agency products should reduce the dispersion in PDs more than the dispersion in LGDs.

Fourth, independently of information problems, banks have greater scope to disagree among themselves about LGDs relative to PDs.[14] The U.S. Basel II Rule provides a clearer definition of default as opposed to the definition of LGD, and so banks should disagree less about PDs than about LGDs. Moreover, differently from PDs, LGDs depend heavily on troubled loan collection and work-out, which vary across banks.[15] Araten (2012) discusses some of these institutional details in depth.[16] He notes that placing borrowers on non-accrual status is a discretionary action, and firms that are more aggressive with identifying loans as non-accrual will have lower expected LGDs, as more loans will report zero LGDs. Banks also vary with regard to how they treat very small exposures, such as loans under $50,000. These loans typically have high loss rates, and a decision to include them in reference data will increase LGDs. Also, banks vary with regard to other policies, including how they treat collateral applied before default and changes in collateral status, how they choose interest rates to discount cash flows, and how they allocate cash flows with multiple exposures to the same borrower. All of these policies, which can be legitimate under the Basel rule, will affect LGD. Thus, the true LGD of a loan could in fact vary across banks, and banks would then diverge on the LGDs that they assign to the same loan for legitimate reasons, which are unrelated to systematic bias by some banks.[17]

---

[14] We thank Mark Levonian for pointing out some of the issues discussed in this paragraph.
[15] If LGD estimates included all costs of loan collection and work-out, then the dispersion in LGDs that we observe might be lower, because banks must invest to collect more value from defaulted loans. However, these costs are most likely not fully captured in the loss data. Still, these costs should not be capable of explaining all the dispersion in LGDs that we estimate.
[16] See also Schuermann (2004) for a discussion about how loan characteristics affect LGDs.
[17] Some of our results might also be explained by differences in the frequency of parameter updates across banks or between PDs and LGDs. If banks differed on the dates in which they update LGDs, then we should observe – as we do - some banks with LGDs systematically higher than other banks, for instance because macroeconomic conditions that affect LGDs might have changed between the dates in which different banks set their LGDs. Indeed, economic conditions were changing rapidly when our data on risk parameters were collected. Also, if PDs were updated more frequently than LGDs, then the differences in the frequency of updates should cause smaller systematic differences in PDs across banks than in LGDs, and we should observe – as we do – little evidence of systematic differences in PDs across banks. Indeed, this reasoning is supported by evidence that macroeconomic

Figure 3 shows the joint distribution of the systematic differences in banks' estimates of PDs and LGDs from our regressions — that is, the points on the graph represent the combination of bank dummy coefficients in Column 1 of Tables 4 and 5 for each bank. The PD is measured by the horizontal axis and the LGD by the vertical axis. As shown in the inset box, the correlation between the estimates for PD and LGD is very low, equal to -0.11. This implies that a bank that systematically reports lower estimates of one parameter is almost equally as likely to report either higher or lower estimates of the other parameter. Given this evidence and the larger number of statistically significant bank dummies in the regressions using LGD as the dependent variable relative to PD, the next section focuses on differences in LGDs.

4. Impact of Inconsistencies in Risk Parameters on Basel II Minimum Required Capital

In this section, we investigate how the systematic dispersion in LGDs estimated in the previous section affects the Basel II minimum regulatory capital that banks must hold. We estimate the impact of differences in LGDs on regulatory capital using the AIRB formula of capital requirement for corporate credit exposures:

$$K = \left[LGD \times N\left(\frac{N^{-1}(PD) + \sqrt{R} \times N^{-1}(0.999)}{\sqrt{1-R}}\right) - (LGD \times PD) \right] \times \left(\frac{1+(M-2.5)\times b}{1-1.5\times b}\right), \qquad (2)$$

where K is the Basel II minimum capital requirement for non-defaulted exposures, $N(.)$ is the cumulative normal distribution function, $N^{-1}(.)$ is the inverse cumulative normal distribution function, R is the correlation factor, M is the effective remaining maturity of the exposure measured in years, and b is the maturity adjustment. Both R and b are functions of PD that take positive values only and are defined in the U.S. Basel II Rule.[18] The dollar risk-based capital requirement for each exposure is calculated by multiplying K by the EAD of the exposure. The formula is linear in LGD, so dispersion in this parameter has a directly proportional effect on

---

conditions affect corporate default rates and credit losses and spreads (Pesaran, Schuerman, Treutler and Weiner, 2006; Duffie, Saita and Wang, 2007; Bonfim, 2009; Lando and Nielsen, 2010; Tang and Yan, 2010; Jacobson, Lindé and Roszbach, 2013). However, we believe that differences in the frequency of updates cannot explain our results, because Basel II rules require that banks validate PDs and LGDs on at least an annual basis.

[18] See Table B on page 69335 of Office of the Comptroller of the Currency, Board of Governors of the Federal Reserve System, Federal Deposit Insurance Corporation and Office of Thrift Supervision (2007).

dollar risk-based capital requirement. Thus, the linear relationship makes it straightforward to calculate the effect of the dispersion of LGDs on capital requirements.

According to Column 1 in Table 5, the lowest bank dummy is -12.79 and the highest bank dummy is 17.44, which imply differences of -12.79 and 17.44 percent from the median bank's LGD, respectively. The median LGD in our sample is 40.70 percent. If the median bank assigned this LGD value to a loan, the bank with the lowest dummy would assign to the same loan an LGD of 27.91 percent, and the bank with the highest dummy would assign an LGD of 58.14 percent. We assume that all other risk parameters in (2), including PD, are constant across banks. Our findings imply that, if all banks had the same portfolio of loans, then the bank that sets the highest LGDs would be required to hold approximately twice as much capital for regulatory purposes as the bank that sets the lowest LGDs. Thus, the differences in LGDs estimated in the previous section could have a strong impact on Basel II minimum regulatory capital.

However, we note that this dispersion does not necessarily directly translate into banks actually holding less capital. First, because the Basel II minimum requirement is typically not binding for banks, except in times of extreme stress. Also, because U.S. banks must exit parallel run to use these LGDs and, as of the time of writing this article, no U.S. bank has exited parallel run yet. Still, these differences remain important for at least two reasons. First, Basel II regulatory capital requirements are used by regulators and the market to assess bank risk. Second, the Fed uses PDs and LGDs estimated by banks for other types of loans, such as real estate loans, in the Comprehensive Capital Analysis and Review (CCAR), popularly known as the Stress Test, which has important implications for banks.

5. Risk Parameters and Loan Shares

In Section 3, we showed that banks differ systematically in the LGDs that they assign to loans. We also argued that these differences can be potentially explained both by differences in the losses that banks expect to incur in case these loans default and by differences in how banks estimate LGDs that are unrelated to the losses that they expect in case of default. These two possible explanations imply different relations between LGDs and loan shares: If LGD differences are caused by expected losses, then LGDs should be negatively related to loan shares, because banks would prefer loans with low LGDs; if LGD differences are unrelated to expected losses, then LGDs should not be correlated with loan shares, because banks would be indifferent about LGDs. In this section, we investigate empirically the relation between LGDs and loan shares.

5.1 Empirical Strategy

We estimate the following regression:

$$Z_{ij} = X_{ij}\beta + \gamma_i + \delta_j + \varepsilon_{ij}, \qquad (3)$$

where Z_{ij} is the share of loan i held by bank j, X_{ij} is a vector of characteristics specific to each loan-bank pair ij and β is a vector of coefficients. γ_i and δ_j are vectors of loan and bank dummies, respectively, and ε_{ij} represents an unobservable error specific to each loan-bank pair. The vector X_{ij} now includes the PD and the LGD that bank j assigns to loan i. Again, we estimate robust standard errors and we cluster observations at the loan level. We use a truncated regression model to account for the fact that the dependent variable, loan share, is strictly bounded from below by zero.[19]

5.2 Results

Table 6 shows the results of our analysis. We limit our analysis to the 891 loan and bank pairs that do not have missing data on loan share. Column 1 shows the results for the full sample. Higher LGDs have a negative relation with loan share, while PDs do not. The effect is large: an increase in LGD of 100 basis points is associated with a decrease in loan share participation of

---

[19] It is also bounded above by 100, but no bank in our sample has a share close to that number.

262 basis points. As these loans involve hundreds of millions of dollars, even small shifts in loan share imply significant changes in exposure.

In Column 2, we investigate if the relation between LGD and loan share depends on information asymmetry about borrowers. This relation might be stronger for loans extended to opaque borrowers, for instance, because banks typically find it harder to monitor these borrowers, and thus banks might believe that these loans are more likely to default. To investigate this, we again separate borrowers between opaque (private or public nonrated firms) and transparent (public firms rated by Moody's or S&P). Also, we group private and public nonrated firms together in the opaque category, as we did in Columns 4 and 5 of Tables 4 and 5. We create a dummy variable that is equal to one if the borrower is an opaque firm, and equal to zero if it is a transparent firm. We measure the difference in the impact of PDs and LGDs between loans to opaque and transparent borrowers with two terms, which interact PD and LGD with the opaque dummy, respectively. Once again, we do not find any evidence of a relation between PD and loan share and we find evidence of a strong relation between LGD and loan share. Also, the interaction term of LGD and the opaque dummy indicates that the effect of LGD is largely due to opaque borrowers.

We perform one more robustness tests of the result in Column 1. In Column 3, we study if this result changes if we control for the impact of the loan on the credit risk of bank's loan portfolio. We estimate the marginal contribution of a loan to the bank's credit risk using the method described in Servigny and Renault (2004) and Ivashina (2009). We include the credit risk contribution of a loan the bank's loan portfolio in Column 3, and we find that it does not have a significant effect on the relationship between loan share and risk parameters.[20] Again, the relation with loan share is not significant for PD and large and significant for LGD.

---

[20] We use historic information on defaults by industry to create a covariance default matrix, and then calculate expected default probabilities at the portfolio level for each bank in our sample, using data on their overall syndicated loan portfolio from DealScan. We then assume a 10% loan share participation level, and estimate the marginal contribution of each loan in our sample to the bank's overall default risk, controlling for cross-industry correlations. Unlike Ivashina (2009), we find that loan share has a positive, but insignificant, association with the marginal credit risk variable. We hypothesize this may be due to differences in sample. Ivashina (2009) considers lead arranger share, while we consider all syndicate member banks' shares. Lead arrangers may have different

We also find that banks that lead the loan syndicate, that have participated in past loans to the borrower, or that have led a loan syndicate for the borrower, are likely to hold a larger share of the loan. This finding is robust across specifications and is consistent with past work on the importance of relationships in banking cited above (including Fama, 2000). This result confirms past research using different samples of syndicated loans and also corroborates the hypothesis supported by many of these papers that information asymmetries determine loan syndicate structure. Still, we interpret these coefficients with caution as reverse causality is a possibility.

Our findings in this section are consistent with banks participating more heavily in loans that they consider less risky. Thus, these findings suggest that the systematic differences in LGD that we found in Section 3 actually represent differences in the losses that banks expect to incur if their borrowers default on their loans. Still, we recognize that there are at least two alternative explanations for this negative relation between LGD and loan share. First, banks may also be responding to regulatory incentives that require them to hold less capital for such loans.[21] For instance, if a bank convinces its regulators that it should assign to a loan a lower LGD than this bank assigns to similar loans, then this bank has an incentive to hold a larger share of this loan, even if this bank believes that this loan is not safer than others in its portfolio. Second, there may be reverse causation between LGD and loan share, as banks have a stronger incentive to reduce the LGDs of the largest loans in their portfolios. This happens because the amount of capital that banks must hold for loans is proportional to LGD and to the exposure at default (EAD).[22]

These findings also suggest that differences in risk parameters have implications beyond bank capital. Indeed, banks' beliefs about risk determine their criteria to approve loans and the spreads that they charge for loans. If LGDs measure adequately beliefs about losses, then the

---

information sets, and may also hold loans to signal this information. Our results regarding loan share and lead arranger would be consistent with this relationship being important.

[21] See Jones (2000) for a discussion of regulatory capital arbitrage.

[22] Note that banks are not free to set risk parameters as they see fit. Banks' risk parameters must meet guidelines set by both supervisors and the international Basel regulatory regime. Supervisors, including the Federal Reserve and Office of the Comptroller of the Currency, perform regular examination of each bank's process for assigning risk parameters. Within these limits, banks may direct greater resources towards lowering capital requirements where their exposures are greatest.

dispersion in LGDs that we documented should affect bank credit supply too, as the findings of this section suggest. Moreover, risk parameters may affect other decisions from banks, such as the salaries and bonuses that they pay to their staff. Although we do not investigate these additional effects in this paper, our results indicate that they deserve some analysis too.

6. Conclusion

In this paper, we examined the consistency of nine large U.S. banks' PDs and LGDs. We found that banks show significant dispersion in PDs, but for most banks the dispersion is not systematic. In contrast, banks differ systematically in their LGD estimates, and the sizes of these differences imply large discrepancies in Basel II minimum regulatory capital between the banks that assign the lowest and the highest LGDs.

These results leave at least two important questions unanswered. First, why do we find systematic dispersion in LGDs, but not in PDs? Potential explanations include the different data, definitions, and methods that banks use to estimate risk parameters. Indeed, as the AIRB was designed to encourage banks to use methods that accurately reflect their approaches to credit risk, the dispersion in risk parameters does not necessarily mean that banks' AIRB systems are intentionally biased, or that some institutions are unjustifiably conservative or aggressive. Still, additional work is required to determine the relative importance of these reasons.

Second, why should any risk parameters differ systematically? We believe one reason is that banks differ in preferences for risk, uncertainty, and capitalization. Some banks are more conservative in the face of uncertainty and model risk, and are thus not averse to the higher capital charge associated with higher LGDs. Other banks may put a lower 'price' on the uncertainty around LGDs due to data limitations, and a higher priority on appearing well-capitalized. It is difficult to objectively measure those preferences, and our small sample size makes it challenging to compellingly explore such variation even if a good measure were available.

Our findings regarding loan share and risk parameters also bear further investigation. An appropriate instrument could allow investigators to unwind the direction of causality in the relationship we find; if larger loan shares give banks incentives to reduce their risk parameters, or if they invest in loans where their expected risk is low. Of course, both effects may be present, which would be consistent with the large magnitude of the coefficient. Such investigation must await development of a new identification strategy.

Appendix

In this appendix, we study whether observations of loan-bank pairs with large PDs or the functional form that we assume in equation (1) cause the small number of significant bank dummy coefficients in Table 4. In Table A1, we present additional estimates of this equation, but now using different subsamples of the data and a different functional form to describe the relation between PDs and the independent variables. In Columns 1 to 3 of Table A1, we still use the same functional form from equation (1) and Table 4, but we now use only observations with PDs below 1, 2 and 5 percent, respectively. These subsamples do not contain outliers and therefore the estimates using these subsamples can indicate whether observations with PDs larger than 1, 2 and 5 percent cause the small number of significant bank dummies. The estimates in Column 1, 2 and 3, however, contradict this hypothesis. Across these three columns, at most three bank dummies are significant in each regression, exactly the same number as in Column 1 of Table 4. Thus, removing loan-bank pairs with large values of PDs does not increase the number of statistically significant bank dummy coefficients.

In Column 4, we investigate whether the small number of significant bank dummies in Table 4 can be explained by the functional form embedded in equation (1). We now estimate the same regression with the same sample from Column 1 of Table 4, but now we use the natural logarithm of PD as the dependent variable, which may better account for extreme values of PDs, as opposed to the PD in percentage points. With this alternative functional form, only one bank dummy coefficient is statistically significant. Thus, this functional form cannot increase the number of significant dummy coefficients in this equation either. In summary, the evidence from this appendix does not indicate that the large dispersion in PDs is the main cause for the small number of significant bank dummy coefficients in Table 4, even though such dispersion may partially explain this result.

References

Allen, Linda and Aron A. Gottesman, 2006, "The Informational Efficiency of the Equity Market as Compared to the Syndicated Bank Loan Market," *Journal of Financial Services Research*, Vol. 30, No. 1, August, pp. 5-42.

Araten, Michel, 2012, "Sources of Inconsistencies in Risk Weighted Asset Determinations," working paper, JP Morgan Chase.

Bonfim, Diana, 2009, "Credit Risk Drivers: Evaluating the Contribution of Firm Level Information and of Macroeconomic Dynamics," *Journal of Banking and Finance*, Vol. 33, No. 2, February, pp. 281-299.

Brady, Thomas F., William B. English, and William R. Nelson, 1998, "Recent Changes to the Federal Reserve's Survey of Terms of Business Lending, *Federal Reserve Bulletin*, Vol. 84, August, pp. 604–615.

Carey, Mark, 2002, "Some Evidence on the Consistency of Banks' Internal Credit Ratings," In *Credit Ratings: Methodologies, Rationale and Default Risk*, Michael K. Ong (Ed.), pp. 449-467, London: Risk Books.

Dennis, Steven A. and Donald J. Mullineaux, 2000, "Syndicated Loans," *Journal of Financial Intermediation*, Vol. 9, No. 4, October, pp. 321-469.

Drucker, Steven and Manju Puri, 2009, "On Loan Sales, Loan Contracting, and Lending Relationships," *Review of Financial Studies*, Vol. 22, No. 7, July, pp. 2835-2872.

Duffie, Darrell, Leandro Saita, and Ke Wang, 2007, "Multi-Period Corporate Default Prediction with Stochastic Covariates," *Journal of Financial Economics*, Vol. 83, No. 3, March, pp. 635-665.

Elsas, Ralf and Jan Pieter Krahnen, 1998, "Is Relationship Lending Special? Evidence from Credit-File Data in Germany," *Journal of Banking and Finance*, Vol. 22, No. 10-11, October, pp. 1283-1316.

English, William B. and William R. Nelson, 1998, "Bank Risk Rating of Business Loans," Federal Reserve Board FEDS working paper No. 1998-51.

Fama, Eugene F., 1985, "What's Different about Banks?," *Journal of Monetary Economics*, Vol. 15, No. 1, January, pp. 29–39.

Financial Services Authority, 2012, "Results of 2011 Hypothetical Portfolio Exercise for Sovereigns, Banks and Large Corporates," January 25, available at http://www.fsa.gov.uk/static/pubs/international/2011hpe.pdf.

Güner, A. Burak, 2006, "Loan Sales and the Cost of Corporate Borrowing," *Review of Financial Studies*, Vol. 26, No. 6, Summer, pp. 687-716.

Grunert, Jens, Lars Norden, and Martin Weber, 2005, "The Role of Non-Financial Factors in Internal Credit Ratings," *Journal of Banking and Finance*, Vol. 29, No. 2, February, pp. 509-531.

Ivashina, Victoria, 2009, "Asymmetric Information Effects on Loan Spreads," *Journal of Financial Economics*, Vol. 92, No. 2, May, pp. 300–319.

Jacobson, Tor, Jesper Lindé, and Kasper Roszbach, 2006, "Internal Ratings Systems, Implied Credit Risk and the Consistency of Banks' Risk Classification Policies," *Journal of Banking and Finance*, Vol. 30, No. 7, July, pp. 1899-1926.

Jacobson, Tor, Jesper Lindé, and Kasper Roszbach, 2013, "Firm Default and Aggregate Fluctuations," *Journal of the European Economic Association*, Vol. 11, No. 4, August, pp. 945-972.

Jones, David, 2000, "Emerging Problems with the Basel Capital Accord: Regulatory Capital Arbitrage and Related Issues," *Journal of Banking and Finance*, Vol. 24, No. 1-2, January, pp. 35–58.

Lando, David and Mads Stenbo Nielsen, 2010, "Correlation in Corporate Defaults: Contagion or Conditional Independence?," *Journal of Financial Intermediation*, Vol. 19, No. 3, July, pp. 355-372.

Lee, Sang Whi and Donald J. Mullineaux, 2004, "Monitoring, Financial Distress, and the Structure of Commercial Lending Syndicates," *Financial Management*, Vol. 33, No. 3, Autumn, pp. 107-130.

Machauer, Achim and Martin Weber, 1998, "Bank Behavior Based on Internal Credit Ratings of Borrowers," *Journal of Banking and Finance*, Vol. 22, No. 10–11, October, pp. 1355-1383.

Office of the Comptroller of the Currency, Board of Governors of the Federal Reserve System, Federal Deposit Insurance Corporation and Office of Thrift Supervision, 2007, "Risk-Based Capital Standards: Advanced Capital Adequacy Framework - Basel II," *Federal Register*, Vol. 72, No. 235, December 7.

Pesaran, M. Hashem, Til Schuermann, Björn-Jakob Treutler, and Scott M. Weiner, 2006, "Macroeconomic Dynamics and Credit Risk: A Global Perspective," *Journal of Money, Credit and Banking*, Vol. 38, No. 5, August, pp. 1211-1261.

RMA Capital Working Group, "EDF Estimation: A 'Test-Deck' Exercise," *RMA Journal*, November, pp. 54-61.

Schuermann, Til, 2004, "What Do We Know about Loss Given Default?," In *Credit Risk Models and Management*, David Shimko (Ed.), pp. 249-274, London: Risk Books.

Servigny, Arnaud de and Olivier Renault, 2004, *Measuring and Managing Credit Risk*, New York, McGraw-Hill.

Sufi, Amir, 2007, "Information Asymmetry and Financing Arrangements: Evidence from Syndicated Loans," *Journal of Finance*, Vol. 62, No. 2, April, pp. 629-668.

Tang, Dragon Yongjun and Hong Yan, "Market Conditions, Default Risk and Credit Spreads," *Journal of Banking and Finance*, Vol. 34, No. 4, April, pp. 743-753.

Treacy, William F. and Mark Carey, 2000, "Credit Risk Rating Systems at Large US Banks," *Journal of Banking and Finance*, Vol. 24, No. 1-2, January, pp. 167-201.

Figure 1

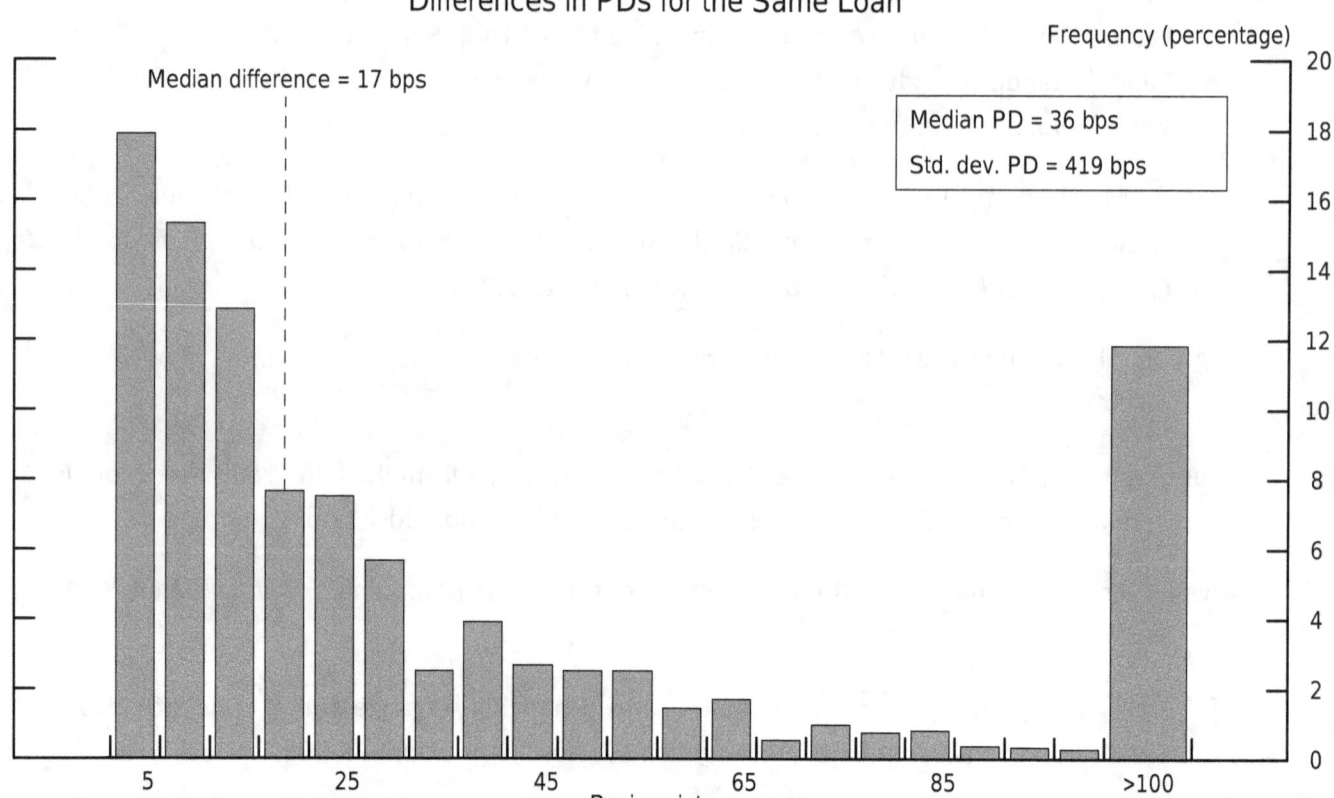

Note: This figure shows the distribution of the absolute difference between PDs assigned by all the 1,868 pairs of banks that participate in the same loan. These differences range from zero to hundreds of basis points, but most are closer to zero. As shown by the dashed vertical line, about half of the pairs of PDs assigned to the same loan by different banks lie within 17 basis points of each other. Still, the median difference across pairs of banks is relatively large compared with the median PD of 36 basis points, shown in the inset box. Moreover, as shown by the right-most bar, in more than 10 percent of these pairs, PDs differ by more than 100 basis points.

Figure 2

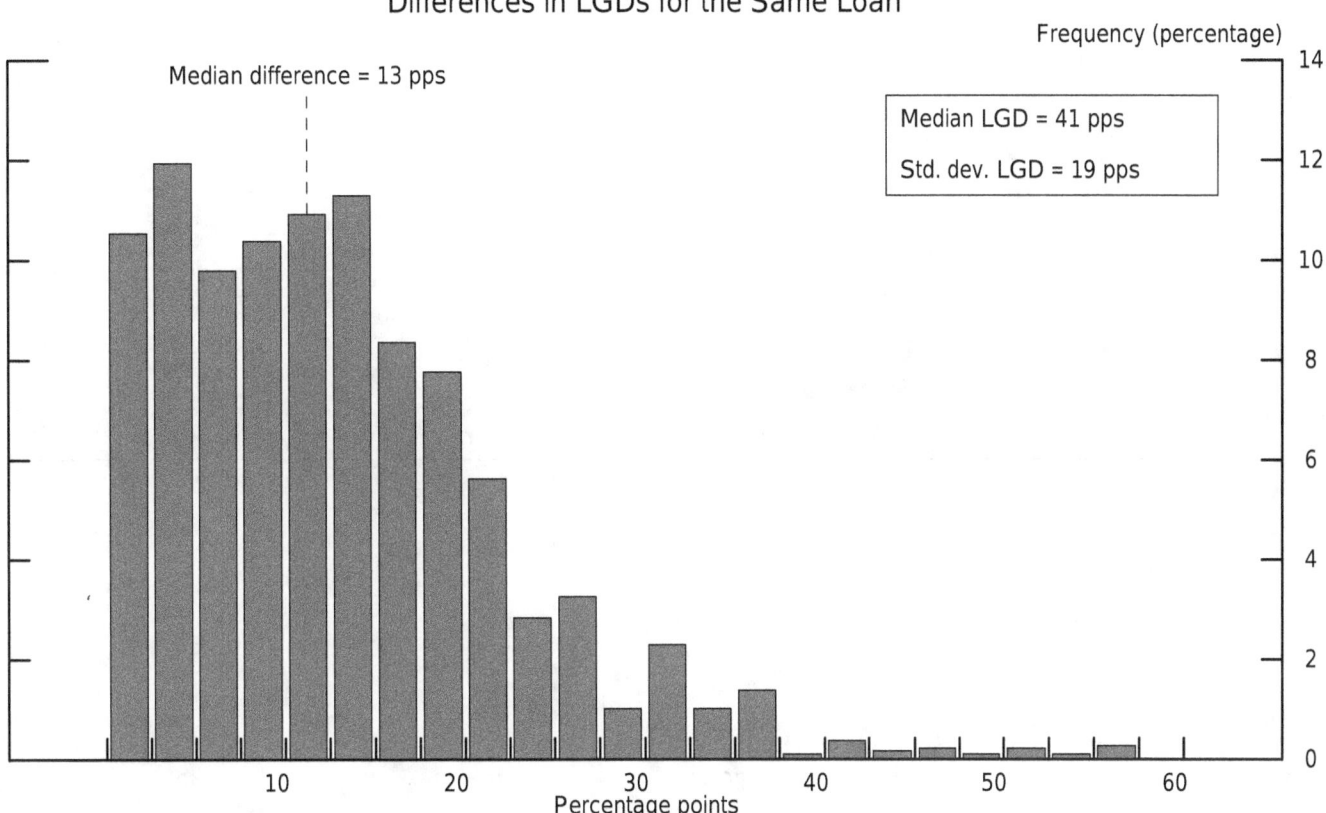

Note: This figure shows the distribution of the absolute difference between LGDs assigned by all the 1,868 pairs of banks that participate in the same loan. These differences range from zero to almost 60 percentage points, but most are closer to zero. As shown by the dashed vertical line, about half of the pairs of LGDs assigned to the same loan by different banks lie within 13 percentage points of each other. Still, that difference is about one-third of the median LGD of 41 percentage points, shown in the inset box.

Figure 3

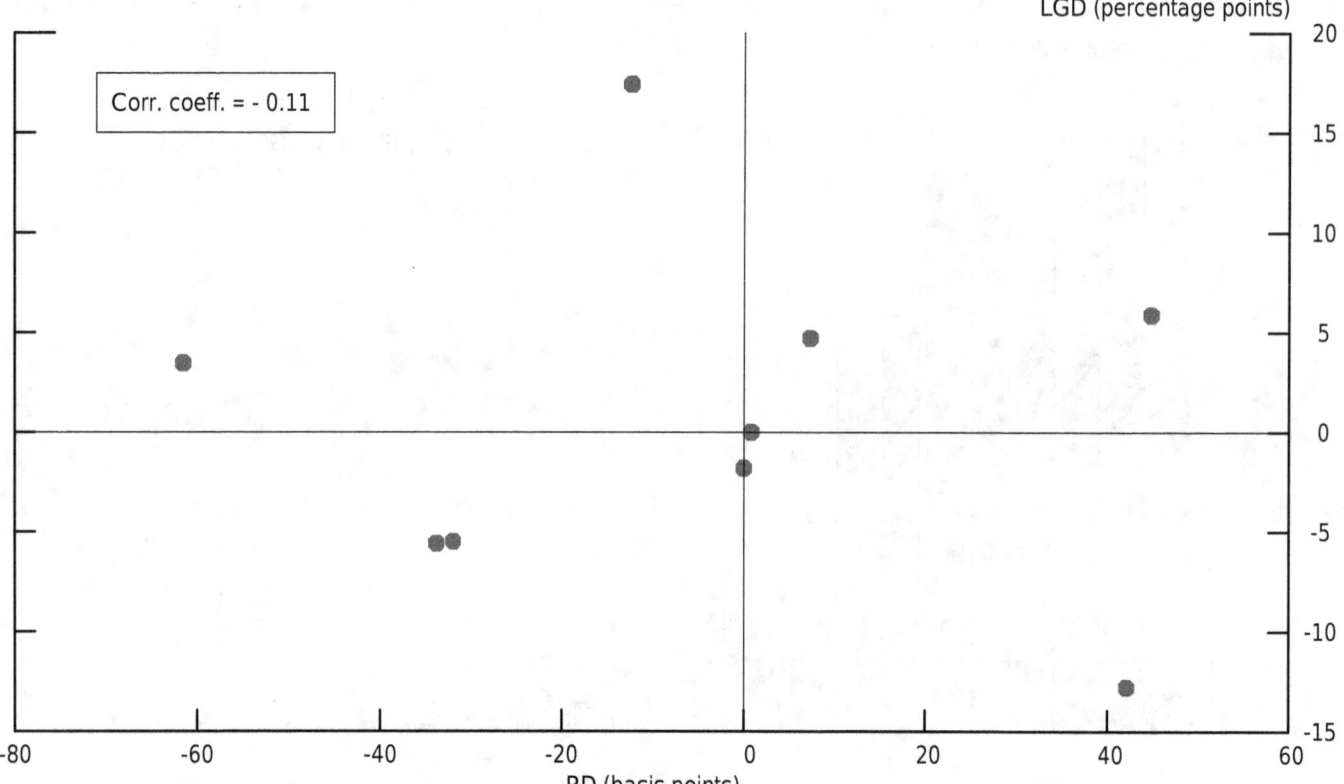

Joint Distribution of Average PD and LGD Differences from Median Bank

Note: This figure shows the joint distribution of the systematic differences in banks' estimates of PDs and LGDs from our regressions. The points on the graph represent the combination of bank dummy coefficients in Column 1 of Tables 4 and 5 for each bank. The PD is measured by the horizontal axis and the LGD by the vertical axis. As shown in the inset box, the correlation between the estimates for PD and LGD is very low, equal to -0.11. This implies that a bank that systematically reports lower estimates of one parameter is almost equally as likely to report either higher or lower estimates of the other parameter.

Table 1: Number of Lenders per Loan

Number of lenders	Number of loans	Percentage of total
2	357	54.17
3	185	28.07
4	75	11.38
5	32	4.86
6	4	0.61
7	6	0.91
Total	659	100.00

Table 2: Summary Statistics of Loans

Variable	Mean	Standard deviation	Minimum	Median	Maximum
Borrower's annual sales ($ million)	8,034	17,033	8	2,739	194,000
Borrower is a public rated firm	62.37				
Borrower is a public nonrated firm	33.84				
Borrower is a private firm	1.67				
Borrower type not reported	2.12				
Loan facility amount ($ million)	817	1,090	25	500	10,000
Total deal amount ($ million)	932	1,120	30	600	10,000
Secured loan	27.39				
Number of loans	659				

Note: Variables are measured in percentage points, unless indicated otherwise.
The percentage of secured loans is based on the 566 loans with no conflicting information from banks.
Total deal amount is larger than loan amount when a deal includes multiple loans.

Table 3: Summary Statistics of Bank-Loan Observations

Variable	Mean	Standard deviation	Minimum	Median	Maximum
Probability of default	1.43	4.19	0.01	0.36	51.56
Loss given default	41.31	12.85	0.10	40.70	81.41
Credit risk contribution	0.00	0.01	-0.01	0.00	0.14
Syndicate leader	25.01				
Past leader	27.58				
Past participant	78.38				
Number of observations	1,795				
Number of loans	659				

Note: Variables are measured in percentage points.
A loan is counted multiple times if multiple lenders participate in it.
The number of observations of "credit risk contribution" is 1,773.

Table 4: Determinants of Probability of Default

Variable	(1) Full sample	(2) Small borrowers	(3) Large borrowers	(4) Public rated	(5) Public nonrated or private	(6) Secured loans	(7) Unsecured loans	(8) Low Moody's rating	(9) High Moody's rating
Syndicate leader	-0.111	-0.474*	0.200	-0.056	-0.236	0.520	-0.184	0.361	-0.139
	(0.177)	(0.229)	(0.248)	(0.242)	(0.270)	(0.694)	(0.144)	(0.565)	(0.210)
Past participant	0.106	0.019	0.201	0.258	-0.098	0.008	0.155	-0.187	0.598
	(0.183)	(0.163)	(0.343)	(0.288)	(0.206)	(0.379)	(0.267)	(0.322)	(0.651)
Past leader	0.212	0.217	0.285	0.163	0.404	0.448	0.044	0.846	-0.051
	(0.218)	(0.235)	(0.359)	(0.297)	(0.337)	(0.865)	(0.162)	(0.594)	(0.214)
Bank 1 (lowest)	-0.616*	-0.481	-0.930	-0.791*	-0.808	-1.718	-0.296	-1.576	-0.240
	(0.287)	(0.551)	(0.534)	(0.339)	(0.610)	(1.038)	(0.207)	(0.852)	(0.232)
Bank 2	-0.333*	-0.295	-0.308	-0.100	-0.691	-0.786	-0.192	-0.408	-0.172
	(0.168)	(0.566)	(0.237)	(0.305)	(0.393)	(0.429)	(0.225)	(0.356)	(0.277)
Bank 3	-0.325	-0.224	-0.298	-0.086	-0.456	-0.371	-0.167	-0.143	-0.171
	(0.224)	(0.569)	(0.357)	(0.249)	(0.335)	(0.377)	(0.129)	(0.510)	(0.357)
Bank 4	-0.123	-0.065	-0.020	-0.056	-0.055	-0.176	-0.158	-0.087	-0.120
	(0.140)	(0.475)	(0.187)	(0.353)	(0.426)	(0.628)	(0.132)	(0.235)	(0.292)
Bank 5	0.008	0.001	0.087	0.050	0.011	0.087	0.043	0.044	0.024
	(0.234)	(0.515)	(0.143)	(0.282)	(0.436)	(2.167)	(0.287)	(0.269)	(0.292)
Bank 6	0.073	0.421	0.176	0.063	0.012	0.156	0.094	0.240	0.027
	(0.218)	(0.633)	(0.220)	(0.379)	(0.232)	(0.427)	(0.144)	(0.690)	(0.294)
Bank 7	0.421	0.487	0.220	0.647*	0.117	1.827	0.196	1.007	0.076
	(0.290)	(0.521)	(0.416)	(0.284)	(0.324)	(1.135)	(0.151)	(0.598)	(0.459)
Bank 8 (highest)	0.448*	0.685	0.530*	0.726*	0.465	2.102**	0.235	1.126**	0.158
	(0.180)	(0.882)	(0.262)	(0.323)	(0.628)	(0.689)	(0.322)	(0.384)	(0.215)
Observations	1,795	842	953	1,155	600	382	1,140	548	567
Loans	659	330	329	411	234	155	411	198	198
R-squared	0.029	0.035	0.038	0.045	0.030	0.091	0.017	0.080	0.019

Note: The dependent variable is the probability of default measured in percentage points.
All equations include loan fixed effects. * and ** denote significant at the 5 and 1 percent levels, respectively.
Bank dummies are ordered from lowest to highest in each regression, so bank identity is not constant across columns.
Loans in columns 2 and 3 were extended to borrowers with annual sales below and above $ 2.74 billion, respectively.
Loans in columns 8 and 9 have a Moody's senior debt rating of Baa2 or worse and of Baa1 or better, respectively.

Table 5: Determinants of Loss Given Default

Variable	(1) Full sample	(2) Small borrowers	(3) Large borrowers	(4) Public rated	(5) Public nonrated or private	(6) Secured loans	(7) Unsecured loans	(8) Low Moody's rating	(9) High Moody's rating
Syndicate leader	-1.500	-0.915	-1.979	-1.700	-0.844	-1.513	-1.843**	-1.647	-1.439
	(0.810)	(1.247)	(1.083)	(1.039)	(1.350)	(1.399)	(0.626)	(1.682)	(1.201)
Past participant	0.702	-0.917	2.410	0.768	0.684	-2.588	0.386	2.319	0.613
	(0.898)	(1.209)	(1.351)	(1.023)	(1.774)	(1.972)	(0.580)	(1.660)	(1.009)
Past leader	-1.675*	-1.920	-1.358	-2.137*	-0.691	-0.441	0.232	-3.329*	-1.211
	(0.820)	(1.316)	(1.061)	(1.041)	(1.499)	(1.717)	(0.606)	(1.517)	(1.219)
Bank 1 (lowest)	-12.793**	-12.226**	-12.916**	-12.001**	-14.532**	-7.862*	-13.634**	-9.668**	-12.524**
	(0.908)	(1.722)	(1.041)	(1.054)	(1.849)	(3.062)	(0.741)	(1.572)	(1.017)
Bank 2	-5.584**	-5.172**	-6.500**	-6.434**	-6.056**	-5.385**	-4.068**	-6.470**	-5.047*
	(0.911)	(1.790)	(1.198)	(1.532)	(1.603)	(1.566)	(0.660)	(1.720)	(2.332)
Bank 3	-5.487**	-4.581**	-5.583**	-5.481**	-3.975	-3.517	-2.908*	-4.191**	-4.299**
	(1.235)	(1.399)	(1.711)	(1.154)	(2.228)	(2.004)	(1.307)	(1.174)	(1.306)
Bank 4	-1.824	-2.042	-1.749	-2.378	-1.229	-2.823	-0.468	-0.713	-1.640
	(1.024)	(1.658)	(1.272)	(1.294)	(1.787)	(1.774)	(0.881)	(2.114)	(1.846)
Bank 5	3.444**	2.371	4.859**	4.059**	2.518	2.299	6.786**	1.291	7.886**
	(1.122)	(1.677)	(1.306)	(1.296)	(2.101)	(1.832)	(0.919)	(2.001)	(1.599)
Bank 6	4.718**	4.329*	4.865**	4.831**	4.645	7.925**	11.269**	2.280	9.930**
	(1.106)	(2.164)	(1.398)	(1.334)	(2.381)	(2.062)	(0.629)	(2.376)	(1.338)
Bank 7	5.870**	4.990**	6.480**	6.603**	5.116*	13.960**	12.688**	2.912	12.383**
	(1.320)	(1.895)	(1.863)	(1.620)	(2.311)	(4.133)	(0.787)	(1.944)	(1.521)
Bank 8 (highest)	17.438**	20.175	17.411**	16.440**	18.216**	31.412**	17.492**	24.265**	18.794**
	(1.818)	(10.969)	(1.681)	(2.072)	(2.439)	(1.088)	(1.339)	(5.506)	(2.101)
Observations	1,795	842	953	1,155	600	382	1,140	548	567
Loans	659	330	329	411	234	155	411	198	198
R-squared	0.373	0.225	0.491	0.420	0.290	0.332	0.754	0.218	0.687

Note: The dependent variable is the loss given default measured in percentage points.
All equations include loan fixed effects. * and ** denote significant at the 5 and 1 percent levels, respectively.
Bank dummies are ordered from lowest to highest in each regression, so bank identity is not constant across columns.
Loans in columns 2 and 3 were extended to borrowers with annual sales below and above $ 2.74 billion, respectively.
Loans in columns 8 and 9 have a Moody's senior debt rating of Baa2 or worse and of Baa1 or better, respectively.

Table 6: Determinants of Loan Shares

Variable	(1) Baseline specification	(2) Baseline + interaction terms	(3) Baseline + credit risk contribution
Probability of Default	-0.519	-4.184	-0.235
	(6.261)	(7.737)	(6.240)
Loss Given Default	-2.616**	-0.670	-2.468*
	(0.974)	(1.028)	(0.983)
Syndicate leader	3.631**	3.632**	3.640**
	(0.276)	(0.277)	(0.277)
Past participant	1.429**	1.394**	1.425**
	(0.338)	(0.334)	(0.338)
Past leader	0.869**	0.917**	0.914**
	(0.300)	(0.307)	(0.305)
Opaque x PD		10.499	
		(12.436)	
Opaque x LGD		-4.974*	
		(2.011)	
Credit risk contribution			18.367
			(12.623)
Bank 1 (lowest)	-2.472**	-2.549**	-2.548**
	(0.405)	(0.413)	(0.409)
Bank 2	-1.893**	-1.928**	-2.426**
	(0.590)	(0.620)	(0.749)
Bank 3	-1.383**	-1.585**	-1.474**
	(0.347)	(0.357)	(0.353)
Bank 4	-0.612	-0.573	-0.613
	(0.390)	(0.399)	(0.395)
Bank 5	0.153	0.129	0.191
	(0.315)	(0.318)	(0.318)
Bank 6	0.464	0.449	0.421
	(0.367)	(0.423)	(0.372)
Bank 7	0.478	0.502	0.464
	(0.418)	(0.368)	(0.422)
Bank 8 (highest)	1.085*	1.033*	1.051*
	(0.462)	(0.475)	(0.465)
Observations	891	872	876
Loans	318	311	313
Log pseudolikelihhod	-1,790	-1,753	-1,761

Note: The dependent variable is loan share in percentage points.
We estimate a truncated regression model with lower limit equal to zero.
All equations include loan fixed effects.
* and ** denote significant at the 5 and 1 percent levels, respectively.
Bank dummies are ordered from lowest to highest in each regression, so bank identity is not constant across columns.

Table A1: Robustness Tests of Determinants of Probability of Default

Variable	(1) PD < 1%	(2) PD < 2%	(3) PD < 5%	(4) Ln(PD)
Syndicate leader	-0.012	-0.010	-0.034	-0.051
	(0.016)	(0.029)	(0.041)	(0.055)
Past participant	-0.024	-0.045	0.008	-0.108
	(0.017)	(0.025)	(0.045)	(0.061)
Past leader	-0.012	-0.013	-0.006	0.029
	(0.016)	(0.024)	(0.039)	(0.050)
Bank 1 (lowest)	-0.135**	-0.034	-0.074	-0.246
	(0.016)	(0.029)	(0.041)	(0.148)
Bank 2	-0.064**	-0.029	-0.064	-0.089
	(0.021)	(0.063)	(0.049)	(0.073)
Bank 3	-0.006	-0.014	-0.036	-0.070
	(0.019)	(0.025)	(0.046)	(0.066)
Bank 4	-0.003	-0.010	-0.015	-0.064
	(0.016)	(0.032)	(0.040)	(0.063)
Bank 5	0.019	0.050	0.037	0.040
	(0.020)	(0.033)	(0.049)	(0.060)
Bank 6	0.032	0.067*	0.061	0.045
	(0.021)	(0.032)	(0.065)	(0.065)
Bank 7	0.036	0.067*	0.120*	0.087
	(0.023)	(0.029)	(0.049)	(0.073)
Bank 8 (highest)	0.083**	0.176**	0.184**	0.300*
	(0.019)	(0.031)	(0.044)	(0.068)
Observations	1,458	1,621	1,689	1,795
Loans	579	613	634	659
R-squared	0.121	0.069	0.036	0.043

Note: In Columns 1 to 3, the dependent variable is the probability of default measured in percentage points. In Column 4, it is the natural logarithm of the probability of default.
All equations include loan fixed effects. * and ** denote significant at the 5 and 1 percent levels, respectively. Bank dummies are ordered from lowest to highest in each regression, so bank identity is not constant across columns.

www.ingramcontent.com/pod-product-compliance
Lightning Source LLC
Chambersburg PA
CBHW081808170526
45167CB00008B/3371